Average American

Poems On Becoming Normal

Ty Gardner

For more information, address: gardnty@gmail.com

ISBN: 9798393131623

this is for words

—

Other titles from Ty:

Table of Contents

Birth

birth
/bərTH/

• the beginning or coming into existence of something.

with a blink and a breath, i am beautiful.
fuzz, and gums, and little fingers,
everything in its place, blinking, beautiful.

tomorrow i begin the long road to ugliness,
the period when our gums grow teeth
to sharpen our tongues.

i could nick the skin with a hard question here
or kill a mood with a harsh gaze.

these will be the years i grow legs to run with,
the stolen ones taken from my brother
at the onset of a heart defect.

experience will grant me feet to stand on,
and with time i will plant them firmly.
those will be the years when i am average,
the space between ugliness and obligation.

today, however, i am beautiful.
breathing, blinking, everything in its place.

Youth

youth
/yo͞oTH/

• the period between childhood and adult age.

my youngest may forget this day with time
but ask again when the odd photo surfaces.
a snowless january in the park, i'll say to myself,
musing the wild-eyed dog that knocked
the incisors from his mouth.

he is a child in this age of unprovoked attacks
in the park and speaks almost dismissively
of the response training his school teaches
when an active shooter is on the premises.

i recall endless back-road bicycling
and hours of small-stream fishing
as i think on mine and pray these
are not the things he remembers
when looking back on his.

Love

love
/ləv/

• an intense feeling of deep affection.

the story of my father offering his driver's license
as credit for a pack of diapers to last me the week,
assuring the station clerk that he'll return to square
the bill with his next check comes to mind.

or the early morning deer hunt,
his camo shirtsleeve sopping wet
with fresh mucus from my frigid boyish nose;
fond reminders on the topic of affection,
and i'm often sure that these moments
(tendered in loving resignation)
count as the truest forms of the act.

—as an afterthought,
the recollection of my father and uncle scraping bits
and chunks of blood and guts off of their vehicle
after an over-jealous man attempting to murder
his wife and her lover with dynamite,
blew himself from hell to breakfast,
schleps to the surface now and again
and i think this act, too, could be counted.

Family

fam·i·ly
/ˈfam(ə)lē/

• a group of one or more parents and
their children living together as a unit.

in the end, we were five; my siblings and i.
a mixed bag of imbalances, addiction issues,
and crippling personality disorders.
we toed the line most days but kept our folks
on theirs with fist fights and screaming fits.

football sundays were church.
a cold ale, god, half-time shows a sermon,
and the flat-screen glow our holy pastor.

by the age of being of age we were already grown.
abuse, arrest, and bad habits put the lot
of us through jail or on the streets early—
an education hard-learned through living hard.

in the end, we were five;
a mixed bag of flawed humans toeing the line,
raising our own while trying to be one;
my siblings and i.

Mortality

mor·tal·i·ty
/môrˈtalədē/

• the state of being subject to death.

the tin roof, blue, with louvered shutters to match;
i'd quite forgotten them, i'm afraid.
and the capillary of television cables snaking
their way beneath the eaves, too,
are somewhat foreign to me.

i can tell you of the crack willows, though.
broad as the barn side and full of themselves;
how they taunted my brother and i to infiltrate their
density, snickering their regards as we leapt from the high
branches to escape a hailstorm of hidden black bees.

i can tell you that the back door,
blue now to complement the scheme of things,
once was white with winter grief at the shaggy mutt
taking to his shallow grave feet from its steps.

and i can tell you that we're bound to little details,
the louvered ones buried far beneath the shaggy mutts,
past the nestled bees and snaking cables;
that they're closest to us the further our thoughts move
from innocence and into acknowledgment.

Romance

ro·mance
/rōˈmans,ˈrōˌmans/

• a feeling of excitement and
mystery associated with love.

ten minutes to midnight on a saturday hang and we get
the call: somewhere between the county lines of the
neighboring canyons, my buddy's latest pursuit's been in a
terrible accident but can't say where.
     due north from your town,
    keep on 'til you see the lights,
is the best she can tell us, and within seconds we're
booking toward the freeway, eyes peeled with the
pedal to the floor.

an hour's drive bangs on before the red/blue sounding
board of responder vehicles alert us that we've arrived.
pulling onto the crunch of a gravel paved u-turn,
the full scope of what's happened sets in and it hits us
that a touch of divine intervention or stroke
of immeasurable luck has transpired.

at an eye-popping 110 m.p.h., this girl had pin-balled off
the cement barriers down the weber canyon pass and shot
straight through the u-turn we'd just pulled into, the nose
of her now mangled vehicle pointing directly at oncoming
traffic; the entire ordeal undoubtedly a valuable lesson in
hindsight that several attending officers were pleased to
remind us as we departed.

in the welcome lull of the post kissy/huggy reunion
schmooze i'll happily omit here, it occurred to me that,
with all of my heart, i believed i'd witnessed a true
miracle that evening. two lovers, wholly infatuated and
grateful to the other in the face of uncertainty, had been
blessed with a new lease on their budding relationship
(cue the awws); surely such a thing was powerful enough
to tug the sternest of heartstrings?

well, as these things often go, valley girls from the
boulevard are a dime a dozen, and it wasn't long before
my friend had coupled up with the next wild hair
delivering the 'theater' line from alanis morissette's
"you oughta know" with overtly sexual fervor.

Curiosity

cu·ri·os·i·ty
/ˌkyo͞orēˈäsədē/

• a strong desire to know or learn something.

what we'd hoped to get out of it after the
storage chest was pulled back i couldn't say.
not then, and certainly not now.
fulfilling some innate sense of morbidity if i were to
guess, but it matters very little; bloodstained carpet is a
shade of void so dark it could've swallowed the lot of us—

on that much, we'd all agreed.

Marriage

mar·riage
/ˈmerij/

• the state of being married.

christmas vacation, vegas, tail end of the late 2000s,
five years of contention with my first wife comes
to a head at the drunken suggestion (mine)
we trade sexual encounters with our friends,
an accompanying married couple.

naturally, chaos ensues and,
not for the sake of omission or to keep
the dirtiness of it cast in the same ugly
silence a parent would an illegitimate child,
but because there's far more to tell than
the space of a few paragraphs will allow,
the abridged version is that my illicit offer goes
relatively unrequited, and six hours of four people
inhaling the other's exhaled contempt like a stale fart
embedded in the cloth seats of our sedan as
we drove home is a fairly passable depiction
of the lingering animosity between us.

suffice it to say, by january the next year there was little
else to do but slap my john hancock on the dotted line,
dissolve our relationship and crawl into a dank hole where
i could weather the blue funk a while.

Karma

kar·ma
/ˈkärmə/

• (in hinduism and buddhism) the sum of a person's
actions in this and previous states of existence,
viewed as deciding their fate in future existences.

the score was simple enough: wallet to hand, hand to
pocket, eyes and teeth to cloak my guilt.leisure stroll
here, no beeline movements. steady on through the
peering crowd and i'm home free—simple.

ten feet out the door and i'm pouring over my bounty; an
espresso brown trifold, brimming with cash, gorgeous.

in reality, i'd likely pinched it charcoal black,
zipper pockets with velcro strips, but it must be
remembered that way, heightens the experience, you see?

my point is that the rush enlivens our imagination,
imparting a fleeting sensation of excitement when
the memory is recalled.

what stays with you, though,
the tangible shame inevitably ushering excitement away,
is the pain that wells behind their eyes (your victims),
the quaking desperation in their voice when they
confront you, and the crushing humiliation of the lies
told to protect your pride.

because when you do a thing enough times,
eventually, it becomes natural; an instinct or reflex.
you do a thing enough times without getting caught,
it becomes a compulsion, like a smoker nipping their
nicotine fingertips.

—several years later, a broken heap of tears
and defeat on the floor of my apartment,
i gathered what little courage i could and dialed
my landlord to inform him that several hundred dollars
from my account had gone missing,
that i could not make the rent that month
and to plead for an extension.

Courage

cour·age
/ˈkərij/

• strength in the face of pain or grief.

june 5, 1976, the teton, idaho dam experiences
catastrophic failure during its first filling after
several seeps in the downstream face give hastily
away to a full-scale breach of sweeping terror eighty
billion gallons strong.

thirteen thousand livestock, and eleven people dead.
twenty miles of state highway and over one hundred
homes and farms devastated as free-flowing contents
of the man-made disaster wreak havoc across the land.

—three hundred miles away,
my grandmother listens anxiously for news of her son,
who was meant to have been fishing nearby that day.

reports of death, damage, and disaster filter through
the airwaves in breathy static, her mind and body a bundle
of nerves as the names of missing locals are listed.—

i know these stories and more,
the ones she isn't keen to tell as we pad
the hallowed cemetery grounds of her childhood home:

her second husband, inexplicably taking his
life in the cab of a pickup truck during a
small getaway with friends as they drove.

or the manic-depressive alcoholic third husband
terrorizing his way through far more years of their
turbulent marriage than anyone could have imagined.

i know these stories and more,
and can testify to this woman's resolve.
decades of hardships, loss, and suffering,
but never without smiling regard for others;
never without poise, grace, and warmth,
does she move through this life as we pad the
hallowed cemetery grounds of her childhood home.

Conduct

con·duct
/ˈkänˌdək(t)/

• the manner in which a person behaves,
especially on a particular occasion or in
a particular context.

with a quilted maple top on mahogany body, rosewood
fingerboard, and synchronized tremolo bridge sporting
axis pickups, the ibanez s series electric guitar was my
red ryder carbine action two-hundred shot range model
air rifle; cheap as chip jewelry and just as appealing.

i'd put down every red cent i could along with a bit
of borrowed credit to afford it and thought of
little else as i waited on the instrument's arrival.

around this same time, my then-girlfriend and i
had arranged for a lovely afternoon together in the city
—full accommodations—
followed by a visit to a beloved school friend's grave.

having seen not hide nor hair of my much-anticipated
purchase in the weeks leading up to our big day
(my frustration increasing with the puzzling holdup),
i decided, rather abruptly to cancel our plans and
start back home on the off chance there was any
news or developments.

as curious irony would have it, delivery of the item had
mistakenly gone to an out-of-town neighbor kind enough
to(very coincidentally) have returned said package in my
absence; imagine my delight at this wonderful surprise!

—walking my worn tips down the
guitar's rich mocha form these years later
i am painfully aware of the price of things,
the ones incurred that can't be recouped.

fidelity, for instance; how deeply i drove a wedge
of distrust in that relationship prioritizing material
goods over sincere human connection.

compassion, another (my indifference the sledge
widening that gap). at the end of our relationship she
wept for us both, for the loss, where i could only find
relief in knowing it was for the best.

and as my guitar gently does now what i could not then,
i am painfully aware of the price of things.
integrity, for instance, and the cost of understanding
that cheap material goods can wait
where sincere human connection cannot.

Work

work
/wərk/

• a task or tasks to be undertaken;
something a person or thing has to do.

graveyards at the old food plant were a bit like how they
sound: skeleton crews of fatigued souls shuffling about
their routines, one menial task to the next in overlarge
steel-toe boots; flunkee types, half-dead, slugging out
the gong show every evening.

one such fellow, the 'old man' we called him, hard as bark
and twice crusted, had been a staple at the place since it
opened in '87. by the time i took nights running a forklift
for third shift, he'd been through the gambit of pinned
knees, spinal fusions, and a bevy of other band aid fixes
that kept the guy in pills.

ten long takes around the sun i watched him lapse
physically and mentally from lack of sleep and crippling
pain, the latter provoking the former and vice versa;
all while providing sole care for a mother and father
unfit to look after themselves.

thirty years he gave. hard ones, late hours on his feet;
the kind that can alter a person's constitution. the old
man was tough, though, stalwart. american bred by folks
pooh-poohing their way through a cocktail of dementia
and cancer, dying the way bad habits do.

tough, as i said, knew what needed doin' and did it.
even earned himself a steak dinner and certificate
of appreciation from the company when he retired—
i thought at length about that later when giving my
two weeks' notice.

Pride

pride
/prīd/

• a feeling of deep pleasure or satisfaction derived from one's own achievements, the achievements of those with whom one is closely associated, or from qualities or possessions that are widely admired.

—this part is passed down from my father, though i do not think it genetic; characteristic, perhaps, a quirk or lifelong habit i've adopted, but entirely unique to him.—

the movements are subtle, inconspicuous,
marginally visible to even the observant eye—subtle.

it might begin with a freckled hand massaging discolored patches of an old elbow wound or the coaxing of foliating neck scruff, but, without fail, my father's palms will take their mark at the tip of his hips, belly protruding slacked shoulders as his eyes narrow with concentration—
the unmistakable tell that you have this man's attention.

and when you have it fully, undivided, the slightest crane of his jaw, a light tilting of his head (to the left, always), serves as a cue that something rare and beautiful will soon take place.

slowly at first, then by degrees, a distant glimmer of amusement softens the bristly fibers of his brows, hiking up the breeches of his upper lip in turn.

it's the faintest smiling exhale through his nose,
however, that truly completes the ensemble;
a fleeting moment of hearty regard for what excites you.

Neglect

ne·glect
/nəˈglek(t)/

• the state or fact of being uncared for.

sissy would've been a grapefruit, honeydew, or
watermelon maybe (papaya-sized, we'll say for
brevity's sake), but i digress. sissy wasn't hair and
bone on the bad days dry with rife like winter hands.

i rubbed my belly copper raw, then, no one cared if i'd
missed a bath. learned where i shouldn't set my foot
down on the minefield of puppy piss and waste that
was my bedroom floor, and discovered the rigor-mortised
remains of our gerbil after spray-bottle spritzing his idle
body out of cruelty more so than concern.

sissy would've been a growth chart fruit through
much of that, but had her bad days just the same.
she was people-sized when her heart decried her
brother's indifference, the older one distracted by
his wash routine and not the feelings minefield that
honeydew had grown into.

she was hair and bone then.

Change

change
/CHānj/

• become different; be altered or modified.

this story, with fairness, is not about the young lady
in the sex film; the secret one long-buried in a cardboard
banker's box with a cache of other unscrupulous home
movies a grieving mother hadn't the heart to throw out.

it is not about how we jeered and rubbed our crossed legs
greedily at that mother's son and the aforementioned
young lady thrumming in the glow of his handycam's night
vision mode as we replayed their comically juvenile
performances, nor the anger we felt when she laughed
off his suicide months later.
　　　　　"compensation for our private little viewing,"
she'd called it—that part we'd put in our own banker's box.

this story isn't about that young lady catching the
smarting side of her cop father's lawful hands several
years later either, before she upped sticks and moved to
the southern desert where no one heard from her again.
this story, with fairness, isn't about any of that.

some of us are big to-dos now, doctors and finance
experts, etc. some of us are family types with sons of our
own, doing the best we can to keep them on the straight
and narrow, sorting through long-buried banker's boxes
and understanding that we're better for the bad things.

and i think, maybe, that is what this story is about.

30

Loss

loss
/lôs,läs/

• the fact or process of losing something or someone.

it would've been a wintry day,
sickly pale with oven-crisped leaves clinging
to slumbering arms when i broke the news;
though i suppose that part's not quite true,
the simplest versions of things are often much harder
to accept, so it stands to reason i'd rather not recall
the unpleasantness of that day any other way.

Fate

fate
/fāt/

• the development of events beyond a person's control,
regarded as determined by a supernatural power.

death keeps a close detail, like a bald fade or buzz cut;
putters around in an apple green cutlass supreme,
seat back with an elbow on the door panel circling
my neighborhood all day long until i leave the house.

where i go, death follows.
i've seen the signs, observed its work for years;
nothing terribly serious, arbitrary reminders
there's nowhere it can't find me—
close like a buzz cut.

several times in recent years,
death has flaunted its presence,
little check-ins i presume;
breathy, like a silent pervert through
the phone before the welcome tune
of the disconnect tone interrupts the line.

sometimes, death brushes a bony
index the length of my spine,
real dainty-like, but discernible.
other times the icy clasp of a firm grip
cupping my nape startles an involuntary
about-face front kick with no one on the receiving end.

it's in these brief exchanges that i afford myself moments of frightening reflection: the woman thrown headfirst through her windshield, ejected at the behest of a stone wall she'd veered her car into as my wife and i walked our dog in the early hours. or the stained matter of a school friend's self-inflicted mortal head wound buried in the fibers of his bedroom carpet.

where i go, death follows,
keeps a close detail and knows my mortal reflections;
the ones i can't stave off when evening's shadow settles
and i'm left to wonder how and when my time will end,
peeking nervously through the blinds at that godforsaken
cutlass puttering down my street, the soft ember glow of
death's cigarette hovering in the dark.

Regret

re·gret
/rəˈɡret/

• a feeling of sadness, repentance,
or disappointment over something
that has happened or been done.

tenth-grade english, i turned in a paper, "the idiot and the
dishwasher," about an alzheimer's sufferer who had added
a touch more soap than the amount recommended to the
detergent dispenser in a moment of admissible confusion,
describing in detail the hilarity of watching this person
scramble to address an ever-advancing sea of sudsing
froth ebbing tide from one corner of the kitchen linoleum
to the other; rightfully so, my teacher had disdainfully
black-marked the paper as reprehensible, a failure by all
accounts much to my surprise at the time.

some years later, splitting hairs to say two decades but
that'll do it right enough, aiding my grandmother in
clearing away the muck and mire at the hearth of her late
husband's headstone, i take penance for omitting
mistaken responsibility in the soap debacle of my youth,
for letting this misfortuned soul take the fall so long ago
and slighting humor publicly.

lovingly, i dirty my hands to cleanse more than polished
marble, but deeply remorseful childish depravity.

Circumstance

cir·cum·stance
/ˈsərkəmˌstans/

• a fact or condition connected with
or relevant to an event or action.

november 18, 1954, ona mae hansen joins one james
francis in holy matrimony. she is clawson strong, good
stock, born up from the dirt her people tempered yet
refined. an honor student, active in drama and music,
ona's prospects are plentiful, her future bright and full
of endless possibilities.

february 17, 1955, precisely one day before their three-
month anniversary, ona mae is struck in the head by the
broken drive shaft of a saw while working with her
husband and father-in-law on their family farm.
this tragic mid-day accident fractures ona's skull
killing her instantly; she is eighteen years old,
and this is where her story comes to an end.

six years pass before jim francis remarries, three more
until my father is born, another twenty from there, and the
cycle continues; with a blink and a breath, i am beautiful.
fuzz, and gums, and little fingers—everything in its place,
blinking, beautiful.

the ending of ona mae's story that fateful day marked
the beginning for many others, like a chipped windshield
fragmenting with winter's chilly influence, and so it is
incumbent that, although our histories may not be shared,
i am mindful of how we are connected so that through
mine, hers will continue to be told.

Reflection

re·flec·tion
/rəˈflekSH(ə)n/

• serious thought or consideration.

better things would be better;
better things would be better than thumbing my
mobile keyboard like a man possessed,
troweling away at the demons deep-sixed,
hoping for some semblance of personal revelation.

better things would be better,
walking the dog or taking a nap,
than penning the heroin addict who forced an
ex-girlfriend on his roommate and contemplating
why i'd felt so compelled to date her after—
better things would be better than that.

better things would be better,
guest reading for my son's elementary class,
clipping the crape myrtle back from our bedroom window,
than tugging up bogeys circling the boat,
ones with the face of my uncle's abuser,
wondering if there's a poem there—
better things would be better than that.

better things would be better;
better things would be better than giving my time to
demons deep-sixed—the poet's bane, perhaps, or just a
man overcome with boredom? better things would be
better than that.

Forgiveness

for·give·ness
/fər'givnəs/

• the action or process of forgiving or being forgiven.

i saw five years between us, pockmarks and tobacco
teeth; another reason to hate him and dislike her
for lying to me.

i saw our lives being upended for excuses i didn't buy,
saw our old home get smaller from the backseat as the
new one came into view.

i saw my fists clench with anger the first time we took
a "family" road trip, saw everything i wanted to see
because he was a kid, like me, and she was old enough
to know better.

i saw other things too, later, when i'd had my own age of
pain; saw that young man being terrified of playing father
to another with angry fists who towered over him.

i saw the woman i'd grown to dislike as my mother
for the first time with pockmarks of her own, looking to
escape a loveless marriage plagued by mangled drywall.

i saw how some things exist outside the black and white,
that we lie to protect the ones we love.

in the end, i saw her humanity because i'd been to war for
my own.

Faith

faith
/fāTH/

• strong belief in god or in the doctrines of a religion, based on spiritual apprehension rather than proof.

just once, the summer of my nineteenth birthday, crossing the parking lot into the park city retail store i worked for, when a softness on my right shoulder, and a familiar voice from behind hastily prompted i come about and face the person addressing me, did i ever genuinely long for truth in the divine.

how readily i'd have traded all my nothings' to pirouette my heels then and know my friend alive and well, shake his hand again, again, then pull his embrace close to mine.

Bias

bi·as
/ˈbīəs/

• prejudice in favor of or against one thing,
person, or group compared with another,
usually in a way considered to be unfair.

in a fit of ill-temper, it isn't beneath me to upbraid snarky
gas station clerks on their choice of employment,
then scowl a response to my wife's reminder
that i'm our stay-at-home parent.

other days i might shoot an off-cuff remark at a
stranger's rhinestone-covered steering wheel,
something unseemly along the lines of trailer-park
royalty as i crank over a cold start in my used xterra;
nothing in earnest, really, but a kill-time activity to
ward off impatience.

and if, on the strong chance, i am feeling particularly
portentous, i'll smirk my brows smugly at all the self-
important bourgeoisie dressed to the nines in my
local walmart combing through the clearance rack.

Empathy

em·pa·thy
/ˈempəTHē/

• the ability to understand and
share the feelings of another.

little marie, with the last name i can't recall,
bless her, piece of work that she was, always picking
at the buttonhole cannulation of her left arm 'til it got
the better of her in the late hours of my dog watch
rounds one evening.

from the shared lavatory between hers and the
neighboring inpatient bedroom i could just make out
their cries for help—little marie and the accompanying
nurse's assistant on duty with me that night.

bursting through from the bathroom side door,
i found the pair of them sheet-white as cartoon ghosts,
a pomegranate-rich pool of blood like a megalodon mouth
breaching the surface beneath them.

six weeks i spent shampooing that carpet, the care facility
too cheap to replace it. little marie kept her finger out of
her shunt from then on, and the poor girl attempting to
help stem the arterial deluge probably only came back to
work there a handful of times afterward.

who could blame her, though? nine bucks an hour with
below-average benefits was an education on the human
condition that afforded us a with-honors degree in
perspective, and i wonder after her sometimes—
the nurse's assistant, not little marie.

Conviction

con·vic·tion
/kən'vikSH(ə)n/

• the quality of showing that one is firmly
convinced of what one believes or says.

newport pier, california, the saltwater stink of it; someone
took our picture there, a shapely being like an edvard
munch painting quietly screaming from the reflection of
our sunglasses. i recall these subtle details upon seeing
the photo now but only then.

that was the year of acknowledging my temporal form and
grieving my lack of legacy.i was angry, often, and actively
distracted; so when a tawny vagrant wearing a "jesus
saves" sandwich board policing the boardwalk shouting at
passersby that, without allegiance to god's will they were
destined for hell, i couldn't help but file the moment most
memorable from that day.

by and by, i came to forget the photo, the contorted
outline warbling in permanent reflection and saltwater
stink, but the tawny vagrant shouting verse and gospel at
the boardwalk reprobates draws my attention even still—
the curious boon of bearing testimony with such exacting
certitude, misguided as i'd thought he was.

a thousand moons have preceded as many suns since
then, and i've come to accept what little time we're
licensed to grieve. active distraction has offered a small
semblance of reprieve, however, in understanding that
wisdom gained from reflection is the only worthwhile
legacy, and that i knew what fate awaited me at my end
the day i found god shouting gospel from the newport
pier in california.

Wisdom

wis·dom
/ˈwizdəm/

• the quality of having experience,
knowledge, and good judgment;
the quality of being wise.

as in proverbs 7:6-9, i, too, once found myself a youth
with no sense, making for the corner drive of a school
crush fancy's country home on a moonless back road
ramble. two and a half wind-nipped miles i wandered
through the threat of a snowstorm squall, wondering
if the weather would hold and whether i was walking
in the right direction.

when finally i chanced upon the residence of the
addressee my heart desired, i hadn't the courage to toss
a beckoning pebble at her window. the looming silhouette
of the family's slumbering creekside estate impressed
little confidence on me that a living soul stirred within,
and hastily i retreated from whence i came.

in muddling defeat, i trudged back to the creature
comforts of my double-wide trailer, visions of a warm
bed coaxing me along. while passing a single-family
cottage off south main, curious movements caught my
weary eye and i paused briefly to peer through the bay-
style aperture where i could clearly discern two sklent
figures, pink with sexual fever, bam-bam in the ham and
groping for trout in a peculiar river.

quick as a wink, i lit a shuck to salt my eyes and burrow beneath a blanket sanctuary. one moment more spent lingering would have been one moment too many, as surely i'd of fainted from sheer embarrassment.

what words of caution i might proffer now in looking back at this faux pas affair, is that the old words still ring true: nothing good ever happens after midnight, only the offbeat not meant for youths with no sense.

so if you find yourself a wayward soul deliberating romantic prospects in the dark noon's ire, at the very least, have the audacity to toss a beckoning pebble at their window!

Brevity

brev·i·ty
/ˈbrevədē/

• shortness of time or duration.

—brief life history of cody ray:
born on 12 june, 1985. lived in heber, utah.
died on 1 july, 2001, aged 16. buried in wallsburg, utah.—

brev·i·ty
/ˈbrevədē/

• concise and exact use of words in writing or speech.

lotta years i spent looking over my shoulder,
cody ray could've crept out from behind
a tetherball pole if he thought for a second
there was an opportunity to terrorize me—
kid had a knack for keeping a guy down;
like a pair of concrete galoshes, he was.

but, in the interest of keeping to the point,
and as an added note of humility
(being that it wasn't me making that left onto highway 40
and catching the grill side of a southbound semi),
it will suffice to close by saying that cody ray was
also an avid outdoorsman with a smile and laugh
missed by all who knew him.

Admission

ad·mis·sion
/əd'miSH(ə)n/

• an acknowledgment of the truth of something.

nights when the rains slap the windows free of their pane,
and i'm meant to be awake, this house is a motleyed stave
of woeful rafters,each with a story to tell.

the collar beams come first, tendering shadows of
coveted things forgotten; hips and lips with curves and
dips, faces not of the mother to my sons.

a jostling of joists, then thresh and bend like demons
writhing. gods, how they howl the day's obscenities,
the musk of my violence perverting our walls,
pleading me penitent to the error of my ways.

it's a caroling of battens foretelling the prophecy
of disappointments yet to come, however,
that rattle their ethereal chains loudest,
challenging the eaves and valleys to sustain
their pitch as the rains steady on.

with the approaching dawn, i concede atonement for
lying in wanting and the volley of verbal assaults cast in
frustration like a net over my children from pain they
can't fathom. a father must lead by example, his heart
on his prospects and not his failures lest the whole of
his roof should buckle and bear down the grave
misfortune of an unremarkable death.

Humility

hu·mil·i·ty
/hyo͞oˈmilədē/

• a modest or low view of one's
own importance;humbleness.

beau's lines and blepharitis, a silver strand here,
another angioma there, each day i choose ugliness;
not for self-effacement's sake, but for preservation's.

every crease and crow's foot is a pen stroke mess of
monostich stories embedded in my parchment cheeks,
a thousand little things to remind myself that i was once
without imperfections, before age liberated me from
youthful ignorance.

Average

av·er·age
/ˈav(ə)rij

• typical; common; ordinary

i

in the summer of my thirty-second season,
on days when the heat index was waft with
turmeric haze and the pressure of conceding
this brief existence had become barometric,
i would lie in the semi-relief of pine shade
to dream of christ in the canonical sense,
how it must feel to be universally regarded,
and question if anything would come of me.
how trite, and seamless, time passed then;
one moment smelting persistently into the
next like the soft watches of a dalí memory.
occasionally, mother melancholy would
whisper sweet nothings' of death's gentle
relief in my ear, depleting my will to live as i
could not grasp what it meant to be human.

ii

deep into cavern's despair i soon wallowed,
darkness driving me ever further from light
to places of silence so clangorous that a cry
for help amounted to little more than faint
plinking of pin drops on a polished surface.
the rhythmic lull of a starless ocean lapped
ominous in absence of lunar affection there,
steadily veering me toward hopelessness.
days oft took weeks to bloom their months,
disinterest's wain signaling no refrain until
somewhere in that breadth of idling swell,
a touch past the point of squinting glimmer,
expression hailed its rousing arms and waved
me on with welcomed gifts in crafting verse.
by way of words, my sentence served warily
in reclusion began to dramatically subside as
inspired and captivating writing manifested
newfound purpose, rekindling a desire to live.

iii

this exciting interim of creativity cultivated
seedling ambition and connected me to other
like-minds moving toward their own beacon.
my prosetic progress escalated nicely in this
community with many encouraging notes of
kindness emerging from all over the world.
verily, providence born of such revival could
fulfill a means to achieve levels of grandeur
eluding me lo these many years, could it not?
i recalled those summer hours spent 'neath
pine shade a-slumber and delighted the love
and ample admiration now inciting my spirit.
adulation, in all of its benevolence, looked to
have delivered away that scape mired in woe,
but at what price steeped in cost too great to
bear remained yet unknown.

iv

the eventual answer to this uncertainty came
subsequent to thirty-seven and some change.
in the lined spaces between these entirely
contrasting chapters, much had transpired;
i lay my most sociable self on the pages here,
courting other dreamers in the quiet hours
where only the floorboards stirred to creak
their due outrage and protest condemnation.
aggrandizing my abilities had instilled an air
of regrettable false confidence within me and,
perhaps as did nazareth's most hallowed son,
i, too, felt the world of iscariots slowly closing
all around at every interval of earnest effort.
sharing myself intimately without reservation
became a judas of heart, and the takers of
things not theirs lined up for a piece of mine.

v

several years of chasing conceit in this way
while shouldering the heft of other's burdens
proved the cross my hands could not hoist,
and i withdrew back into despair once more
to own my guilt and reexamine life's priorities.
pursuing profundity was very clearly just
another form of distraction pulling attention
from those who were most important to me,
and whatever notions i'd previously held on
the subject of becoming noteworthy simply
did not warrant more needless martyrdom.

vi

and so it came to pass that my budding affair
with lady amaranth incurred its final spring.
the whole of my life up to that point could be
insipidly tallied the sum of a series of nouns
defining moments in one requiem to the next.
every dream, each experience, all of my fears,
hopes, wanton needs, and deepest desires,
were merely notes in scales of a syntax symphony,
standing to reason why i'd smacked straight
into the moon rocketing futilely for the stars,
penning the beautiful chaos as it unfolded.

vii

these poems stand now as narratives on
reflected experiences that have influenced
the complex nature of this human condition i
continually try to understand and appreciate,
and i place them here as a reminder that i am
more than the sum of my nouns by accepting
that my work is no longer an undertaking set
on grand designs summoned in a daydream,
but adding together my adjective strengths,
the ones that let us move about unnoticed,
refocused with fresh intent to exist humbly,
my mind off of the past and on becoming normal.

Acknowledgments

To my family, friends, and amazing followers, I must express my thanks and appreciation. Your tireless support inspires me to continue doing what I love, for which I am truly grateful. If my words have reached you or given you pause for a moment of reflection in your day, please, kindly leave a review for this book. Your time and thoughts are important to me.

*A special note of gratitude to Antonia Wang, a dear friend and remarkable poet whose keen wisdom and instincts were invaluable throughout the editing and formatting process of this work; my humblest thanks.

About the Author

A lover of words and the impact they create, Ty Gardner is a lifelong enthusiast of all forms of poetry and has written creatively from the time he was a child.

When he's not musing and waxing poetic, Ty can be found exploring the wonderment of his newfound home in Northwest Arkansas with his family.

He is the author of a dozen poetry books and a co-author of a poetic anthology, *Midnight With Words: Late Night Conversations in Poetry*, along with eleven wonderfully gifted writers from across the globe.

Printed in Great Britain
by Amazon

41069126R00036